Exit Wounds

Caitlin Press Inc.
3375 Ponderosa Way
Qualicum Beach, BC V9K 2J8
www.caitlin-press.com

Text and cover design by Vici Johnstone
Cover image and photograph on pages 3 and 23 courtesy Arfan Ahmed
www.arfansphotography.com
Photographs on pages 32 and 88 from the author's collection
Image on page 60 is in the public domain
Artwork on page 67 by Salman (Sal) Malik

Printed in Canada

Caitlin Press Inc. acknowledges financial support from the Government of Canada
and the Canada Council for the Arts, and the Province of British Columbia through
the British Columbia Arts Council and the Book Publisher's Tax Credit.

Library and Archives Canada Cataloguing in Publication
Exit wounds / Tāriq Malik.
Malik, Tariq, 1951- author.
Poems.
Canadiana 20220215448 | ISBN 9781773861005 (softcover)
LCC PS8626.A44 .E95 2022 | DDC C811/.6—dc23

# EXIT WOUNDS

poems

by Tāriq Malik

CAITLIN PRESS 2022

# Contents

# ~~Entry~~Exit Wounds — 67

# Epilogue — 88

*For Nina—meri jaan, and as always, our Farrah and Salman*

A tongue-firmly-in-cheek Punjabi recipe for cooking a pot (kuji):

Agg phook basantak mera
Gheo te atta tera

I bring the labour and breath
You bring the ingredients

# Foreword

This is an unusual book. As Canadians, especially as British Columbians, we should be well aware of the enormous contribution made by South Asian Canadians to our social, political and economic life. But when it comes to the literary arts, such awareness tends to be more limited. Granted, most of us are familiar with names such as Rohinton Mistry, M.G. Vassanji, Shauna Singh Baldwin, Shyam Selvadurai, and Anita Rau Badami. But they are all writers of fiction. When it comes to poetry written in Canada in English by South Asians, probably the only name that most people would recognize would be Michael Ondaatje's, and then mainly because of his success as a novelist.

True, there have been two well-received anthologies of poetry by South Asian Canadian women, *Shakti's Words* in 1990 and 1993, and *Red Silk* in 2004, which have drawn attention to the work of poets such as Kuldip Gill, Sonnet L'Abbe and Priscila Uppal, but their emphasis, naturally enough, has been on the various roles of South Asian women in the new country. As for individual volumes of poetry, whereas in the USA; poets such as Agha Shahid Ali and Vikram Seth, and in the UK Imtiaz Dharker and Sujata Bhatt have appeared with major publishing houses, by contrast here the work, say, of Ondaatje's fellow Sri Lankan Rienzi Crusz, has been confined to good but lesser-known publishing houses.

However, where Crusz is mainly concerned with negotiating his own personal compromise between his Sri Lankan Burgher heritage and his Canadian experience, Malik seems to know from the start more surely where he belongs, and why he belongs there. But it is not a comfortable place. In the introduction to *Shakti's Words*, their 1990 anthology of South Asian Canadian Women's Poetry, Diane McGifford and Judith Kearns, praise Himani Bannerji's "refusal to separate personal from political concerns." The same could be said *a fortiori* of Malik's work. Throughout a book that, starting with its very title, is much more avowedly political than that of most of his fellow Indo-Canadian poetic contemporaries, he combines a sense of history and a knowledge of myth, not just Indian but also classical European, with events based on his own family's experience and that of his contemporaries.

While as readers we are used to having, say, Shauna Singh Baldwin evoke the bloody aftermath of the assassination of Indira Gandhi, or Tahmima Anam present the horrors of the 1971 war that led to the creation of Bangladesh, there are few comparable examples in Indian English language poetry. So too, with novels from the Pakistani diaspora. Kamila Shamsie in *Home Fire*, Mohsin Hamid in *The Reluctant Fundamentalist* and Nadeem Aslam in *Maps for Lost Lovers* deal directly with such socio-political issues as terrorism, or generational conflict within the new homeland. But for poets it is a very different matter and as far as one can tell from what has been published outside Pakistan there has been no comparable treatment of such issues in the work of diaspora Pakistani poets writing in English or maybe, with the exception of Renee Saklikar's *children of air india,* of any South Asian Canadian poets writing in English.

Overtly political subject matter tends to be problematic for poets. Verse that is written to serve a short-term political end, to act as support for an already held set of beliefs, a cause, *ipso facto* does not reach the level of poetry whose whole purpose is less to proclaim than to explore, to question, to discover hitherto unsuspected connections and establish personal findings which may then prove to have wider significance. It is only too easy to invoke blood, tears, flags, swords, the usual tropes and symbols, for the greater good of a cause, but it requires real genius, such as is shown in two of the greatest English language political poems of the previous century, Robert Lowell's *For the Union Dead* and Auden's *The Shield of Achilles*, to transform anger and disappointment, however justified, into poems that transcend the specific occasion by making the particular representative.

Yet, if Malik's original title for his work, *Nights of Kleptomania*, which refers to imperialist depredations of the lands they conquered, in this case the British in India, makes clear the strong political motivation behind the book, his at times over-emphatic tone is more than balanced out by poems that are rooted in family, in literature and in legend. His main achievement here is to intertwine various aspects of his own domestic life with that of the public events that he evokes, and an alertness to the colonization of language that results from the kleptomania of empire.

Whether he is movingly remembering as a child the death of his father, imagining himself as a dead soldier lost in the sands of the Kuwaiti desert, or drawing upon his own family's experience of "three wars and migrations, and a home invasion," his language is direct and declarative almost in the manner of a fairy tale or a holy text. One senses behind his work a strong oral tradition.

His tone likewise ranges from the outraged to the elegiac, from the celebratory to the fatalistically defiant, so that it can encompass not only traditional Punjabi characters and events, but also the First Nations symbolism of the raven, people falling from the Twin Towers on 9/11, and the RCMP killing of the Polish immigrant, Robert Dziekański, at YVR airport.

This is a book that literally presents a world of experience, critically, angrily and with compassion.

—Christopher Levenson

# First Words

As a first-generation immigrant in Canada, my life here was shaped early by the constant "othering" into a series of creative destructions—highwire acts involving several midair pivots—which at every turn threatened to unravel their apparent grace. This process was further complicated by belonging to a minority that has been racialized and communalized, and finally, due to our uncommon subjectivity, marginalized. One outcome of this has been that there is little or no representation of the newcomer's reality in the dominant social narratives—I have never been made to feel more overly conscious of my skin or with the inflections of my various tongues.

*Exit Wounds* is a debut compilation of fifty poems framed on one very personal narrative—mine and that of my immediate family: we are four individuals who form a "typical" immigrant family. To parse and communicate our experiences, I have modulated the chorus of a billion people in a similar state of flux and amplified a solo: ours. Collectively, we were born in three different countries and have lived and worked on as many continents; we have survived three wars and have been refugees from two adopted homelands. And yet, we are very ordinary in grappling with our multiple dislocations—our pre-occupations having taught us to travel light if we are to discover the truth of our many worlds.

We have now lived willingly in this homeland for over twenty-five years, where, like many others, we are still asked quite often, *but, where are you really, really from?*; or as we may ask each other in our overly familiar idiom: *Boss, where you from?*. As Punjabis, our roots here stretch five generations deep. Yet, our nonrepresentation in the federal and provincial policies and social media has ensured that we remain a relatively new community. I believe that this *"monopoly of the ocean of ink"* in which I am but a drop of blood, must be challenged at every instance, and this book is my groping conceit to fill this void.

My poetics are gleaned from the various cultures I have physically inhabited, namely Punjabi, Urdu, Hindi, Arabic, and English. And if there is a central theme percolating through these poems, beyond the intersectionality of Punjab and the Canadian west coast, it is the search for home, both in the spatial and temporal sense. My work re-examines what racial proximities mean for the plurality of minorities engaging with a dominant atheistic monoculture.

I shall also draw creative parallels with the local indigenous realities and mythologies through our shared themes of speaking in borrowed tongues, and the traumas of our stolen cultures and lands. Like them, I am still searching for my lost tribe.

It has been such a long journey from Kotli to antipodally-located Vancouver in the process of a metalsmith's grandson aspiring to become a wordsmith. Trust me—*there is no single path to crossing a vast chasm in multiple leaps,* yet these leaps of faith will always be original, compelling and universal.

*Decolonize ink!* Stand up and speak these words aloud—poetry must not be read in the dark or silently.

# The Homesick Tribe

The Indian Lohars were gifted metalsmiths who for over 400 years thrived in plying their trade in the northwestern Indian Punjabi village of Kotli Loharan. During the later phase of India's British occupation, the Lohars would emerge from their isolation to face the colonizer's version of the Industrial Age, an age in which local industries were systematically decimated as they offered competition to the British manufacturing back home.

As a result of these policies, within a single generation, the Lohars of Kotli would abandon their workshops and hometown for work overseas and adopt other professions.

The Homesick Tribe is my attempt to capture some of the milieus that the Lohars encountered in venturing out of Kotli.

## The Swimmer of Dunes

*In the aftermath of the Iraqi invasion of Kuwait (1990–1991), several casualties and live land mines were lost to the shifting sands. To this day their exact location and recovery remain elusive.*

Churning between
yesterday                          tomorrow
an annual glacial inch
the growth rate of human nails
this restless landmass
claws its way towards the continent

As temperatures soar
the dune moaning pliant
under the breeze
is on the move again

In the course of one night's looming
several cubic feet of crest
collapse
spilling forgotten hostilities
jumbled down its slopes

Caught in mid-stroke rigor mortis
the swimmer of the dunes
restless and uncharted
dreams at dawn
sifting the residue of sand's insomnia

Once for a decade
my left foot stood exposed
the elements wreaked havoc
while a distant ticking
inched closer

Why does my right shoulder feel so stiff

This blood tastes of rusting nails

## Childhood Hymn

Claiming they have no fresh tears to shed
the professional mourners are the first to go
        and ammiji
        having spent the night murmuring
        to the draped form on the cot
              crumples to the floor
shrouded figures lead her away

Gnarled hands tap my shoulders
        muss my hair
        sound pithy aphorisms
              *You are a man now*
              *Allah gives troubles*
                  *shoulders also*

A month passes
the additional plate is still being set at meals
        before being offered to waiting fakirs
              and vigilant street dogs
        at our bereaved doorsill

By the fortieth day I surprise her
        leaning into the light
fingering a collar stain on a forgotten shirt
        left hanging in the closet

Today
his prized gabardine suit
        is draped on my lanky frame
while she hums to herself
        a familiar childhood hymn

# Creation Story

*(for Satwinder-ji)*

All week long the two hired widows
        a mother and her daughter-in-law
have been shuffling wheat chaff
        from our season of harvest
the sound of their synchronized clapping
        and the thrum and hiss
            of poured seed
        echoing through courtyard and street

When my ammiji teases her
        *Ma why do you insist on working*
        *so late into your dotage*
        *you should be resting at home*
        *and let this one take care of you*
the mother-in-law chuckles

*Bibiji*

        *when Allah kareem sent us down here*
        *he gifted us with a set of twin compulsions*
        *and one straightforward instruction*

Here she points to her belly
        and then glancing obliquely at my rising alarm
the space between her thighs
        *He said now go!*
             *Bandya ja!*
        *spend eternity*
        *crawling on your belly*
        *filling these twin*
             *bottomless*
                 *wells*


*Bandya:* Punjabi for human/man.

## Silenced *Bajra* Voices

*(for Prabhjot-ji)*

We first encounter
      these *bajra* voices
in the millet-grained lyrics of
      folk songs that have yet to see ink

Lightning crackles across distant foothills
      sending thunder rolling onto the plains
         twilight descends

Two girls on the cusp of adulthood
      their hearts too full not yet broken
stand tall facing each other
      sharing a single swing
they sing      *zalima hai ve hai zalima…*
and they sing    *bajray da sitta…*
      innocent yet of the lyrics' intent

As the girls bend their knees in unison
      the swing arches higher with each turn
      the mango tree sways its arms around them
         shedding unripe fruit

A *koel* echoes its fluted call
      the first monsoon drops

Or we encounter *this* boy and *that* girl
      in hide and seek
      where they are the only participants left
         their friends having blended into dark

The boy marvels at the late sliver of day
      fading into indigo
         and how their game has now stretched
         beyond familiar streets and towns
         across dark waters
in an age of kerosene lamps
      telegrams and ocean liners
      before telephones
      before the exchange of first messages

Come out          *come out*
wherever you are whoever you are
            see how everyone has gone out to hide
                    and no one's left to seek them out

## The City Lights of Sialkot

When it is dark enough
our whole family climbs to the rooftop
to witness the unaccustomed glow
          creeping across the southern horizon
marking the miracle of electricity
          inching towards our home
                    to forever blot out our familiar
                         and created stars

Abaji waves at it
          and says one word
               *Sialkot*
he holds my hand tight
          whispering
               *soon soon*

That is the moment
ammiji knows that her other child
          will be a girl
and that she will name her
          *Roshni*
               *Light*

Somewhere in the distance
a steam locomotive sounds its whistle
          the wave travelling ten miles
          over unharvested fields
before striking our home

## The Home Invaded

Ours was to last six war months
leaving indelible bootprints
        across family photos
               scattered throughout

Though lived-in for two decades
        my rented Kuwaiti home I never dreamt you
even when locked out and distant to me
        only desiccated houseplants beckoned
            return

I offer only gratitude to the ignorant and unread
        who took everything else
but spared my books to litter the floor
        their spines snapped

## What We Lost During Our Third War

*Somewhere a bell tolls for our years of war: 1965, 1971, and 1990. Of our involvement in the three wars, we were bystanders in the first, spectators to the next, and then participants in the last. Incidentally, only after the last war were those affected offered any form of reparations.*

Here are some of the items we claimed under UN Iraqi Reparations for the Gulf War of 1990.

1.   A door frame with 15 years of rising height lines
2.   My daughter's second-year shoes
3.   5 favourite Barbies
4.   6 best and battered diecast dinkey cars
5.   VHS tape of my son's first step
6.   A dozen chipped marbles
7.   My wife's favourite Eidh dress—the one she had yet to wear
8.   Black & white negatives older than me
9.   My original *Dark Side of the Moon* cassette
10.  A well-stocked fridge of chilled leftovers from last night's feast
11.  One half of a celebration cake—saved for tomorrow's guests
12.  Months between September and March 1990–1991
13.  That three-star *Shabash!* note of appreciation from a favourite primary school teacher
14.  4.34 years of my estimated remaining lifetime
15.  The lost hours of REM sleep
16.  All my snatched books no longer there for me to interrogate at midnight
17.  Did I list the door frame…?
18.  *(still counting)*

## *Pigeon Feathers* in Anarkali

How could I have walked away
after that first glance at the blurb
        *...some of the best writing in the English language today*
        *is between the covers of this book...*
John Updike's *Pigeon Feathers* is up for grabs
      at this Anarkali sidewalk sale
      of second-hand dog-eared roughly perused books
and it is worth only a *rupiya* and a few *annas*

That single impulsive purchase
      has seen me through a lifetime
three wars migrations and a home invasion
      insolvencies refuges and safe havens

Now it sits in pride of place
      leather-bound
under status: *Hold—Do Not Lend, Ever!*
      on the top shelf of an autobiography
      that is my library

# Star of the Show

STAR OF THE SHOW IMAGE COURTESY ARFAN AHMED

The frock
belonged to a monkey
who bit the show master in the crotch
and was never seen again

*Bachcha Jamura*
now the strongman drawls
pointing at the skinny girl
perched on a platform
the width of her bare feet
atop a ten-foot pole
balanced solely on his thumb

On cue
she gestures at the sky
her glass bangles
clink
the rings on the open palm of the strongman
glint
his gold tooth gleams
as he swiftly hurls the pole several feet vertically
deftly alternating its landing
onto the index finger
*ThaaliyaN*
he repeats
and teases out a reluctant applause

Several times
during this street performance
the girl will scream
the audience will gasp
and a mother cradling an infant in her arms
will move through the crowd pleading
*save my girl      save my poor girl*
*he is going to kill her*
a few in the audience will snicker
unsure if this too is part of the act
so no one will react
until the pole is finally lowered
and the girl with her heart in her mouth
leaps to ground
and is rewarded with applause
The narrow circle tightens around these hustlers
coins are hurled onto a spread sari
and as the strongman retrieves the paltry offerings
while dusting his battered props
the inverted pail begging bowl striped pole

he makes a mental note
*Pity the monkey*

*This skinny four-year-old*
*with feet barely able to perch*
*is already too heavy for this act*

*She is not the star of my show*
*only Raju the master escape artist*
*with slickly oiled locks*
*tumbling down his shoulders*
*escaping all day from successively tighter*
*rings barrels drums boxes*
*takes that honour daily*

The woman who is not her mother
straightens the girl's ruffled frock
while the infant in her arms
an odd series of such infants
squirms
even Tommy the pooch
balancing all day on a rolling drum
descends to earth
as this pretend family
leaves behind the pageant of the city
humming

*Loot leya    loot leya*
*aj assi    mela loot leya*

*Today we looted the carnival*

Heading for their hovels
the infant is returned to the arms of its mother
and the performers pass cotton candy salesmen
and technicoloured dolls
with frilled gaudy dresses
and plastic red slippers

the girl stares at the array of bright balloons

Raju the contortionist
gets to buy a new comb
because he
is

## Eidh in the Time of Covid

Marking the 100<sup>th</sup> day of COVID-19 in Vancouver

In my only village
every measured day
            once equaled a hundred
until a cobra slithered into our home
            devouring its inhabitants
            and all our neighbours
it grew and grew and grew
            swallowing entire neighbourhoods
until it had gobbled up the whole village
            before heading out for city lights

 It is now dark inside here
the crescent is no more
 and we have only
this moment of refuge
 as we gather once again
let's thump each other's shoulders thrice
            and begin one final feast

*This* is what I hear when I am deaf *(hands over ears)*
    *this* is what I see when I am blind *(hands across eyes)*
        and
            *this* is how I scream on mute *(hands across mouth while I scream in the dark)*

"

"

# Suman Bukmun Umyun

*At the graveside of Pakistani Nobel laureate particle physics theorist Abdus Salam.*

The first word was
>> *Read*
and the listener replied
>> *I cannot read*
and the message was repeated thrice
with equal urgency
>> *Read!*

With these first words
>> we began our first journey
we were instructed
>> *Walk gently on the earth*
>> *you are stewards here*
we were reminded that
>> *This earth is a mosque*
>> *and the land beneath your feet is holy*
>>> *Pray anywhere*
>> *In your quest for understanding*
>>> *seek the ends of the world for knowledge*
>>> *even if it takes you to China*

Along the way
we watched the once slim crescent
>> bloom into a branch
>> and then in trimming
>>> retreat into the night
as we aligned our heartbeats
>> to this celestial clock
>> and its rhythms of waxing and waning
until it became ours

Over time we sifted through
>> that first burnt afterimage
>> examining its ash for significance
and sought resonance to
>> connect and prosper
the dervish within us
>> approaching the gyrating vortex
>> learned to whirl inwards
>>> and turn from the looming day

Half a millennium later
        in the twelfth century
the scholar Abu Hamid Al-Ghazali would claim
        *The Quran is all you need*
thus terminating
        our examination of the scientific tradition
Eventually
cramped within the walls
        of our trampled ambitions
*Suman bukmun umyun*
*Deaf blind dumb*
we heard only the intonations of our fears
and with flags unfurled
        launched our protracted marches

What began in one desert
        has come to rest in this distant land
                this land of the pure
        and this grave that is not a mausoleum just yet

Here is a defiled headstone
        where a mere scratch of redaction
        by an anonymous empowered hand
transforms the inscription of
        *… in 1979 became the first Muslim Nobel Prize laureate…*
to read
        *… in 1979 became the first* ▇▇▇ *Nobel Prize laureate…*

See
how the obvious fact left ~~for all to read~~
        almost ceases to ~~exist~~

# Bahadur Singh and the Ballad of Five Rivers

When the land was still young
the rains began
      and lasted a hundred thousand years
and when the waters finally receded
two emerald parrots descended from a rainbow
      one carrying a stalk of wheat
      the other a branch of rice
         and depositing these onto fresh earth
they flew back into the sky

Ever since
determined men on horseback have descended onto this land
      their sights firmly set on its bounty
and for ages men on horseback have risen up to confront them
our folksongs reflect this constant clash
where maidens celebrate the departures and arrivals
      of their men in uniform

>    *… jaana meiN faujiye de naal*
> *paaveN o lath maaray*
> *bootaN naal…*

> *I shall go with the man in uniform*
> *even if he kicks me with his boots*

It is said Punjabis are flamboyant and boisterous
because they have so much to celebrate
and life is too short in this paradise

Such a patch of earth
was inherited by one Bahadur Singh
who
      when provoked in dotage
would proudly respond
      *I still belong to the regiment of five rivers*
      *even if the battles I fought*
      *were other people's wars*
wWhen summoned to
defend the tired bloodlines
      and honour of a distant king who had enslaved us
half a million responded to the call

to hurl endless salvo after salvo
        at an unseen enemy
         and unseen distant targets
we rolled out of dust storms
landless farmers unyoked from our oxen
specks of *Chenaabi* silt drifting on the winds
Rising out of our parched fields
we breathed in the dust smoke
        with every mouthful of cordite ash
and were swept afar and deposited
        to die forgotten
so distant from the graves and pyres
        of our forefathers
self-immolating to belong
        forever to this one spot

We all march daily towards our deaths
only the *jawaan* marches a shorter bitter
        redirected path

Upon my return I spoke incessantly for years
        before falling silent

In another lifetime when I was old enough
my father took me to a seasonal festival
where the highlight was a sunset wrestling match
between two legendary champions
        a skinny one from Punjab
        the other a hefty fellow from the hills

Today
I can still smell the dust kicked up by those titans
        the thunder of their slapped thighs
        the exchanged rebukes echoing
when the wrestlers brought their heels down for traction
        I felt the earth shudder
before the two trundled into locked embraces
        like rutting elephants

Somehow this memory is now muddled
with that of the honour of a distant king
        and the ant armies he summoned
        in making his chess moves across the globe
As light recedes

dew settles the dust
        but the memory of that confrontation
is clouded by loss
        and marked by an immense stillness

I forget now who finally won
        or lost

*Notes:*
*Chenaabi is Punjabi for belonging to the local area of the River Chenaab;*
*Jawaan: Junior soldier (especially a young infantryman) in South Asia.*

# The Last Lohar

*For my Abaji, Suleman Hyat Malik (1919–1973) on his 100<sup>th</sup> birthday*

On this
his final day
the last Lohar
takes a deep breath
and douses the fires of his kiln
absent-mindedly deflating the bellows
tucking them under the workbench
to await a better day

Amidst this final burst of sunlight
he pauses with the unaccustomed leisure
of a summer afternoon
tumbling into
inactivity

The workshops that surround him
have all been boarded up
and the open streets littered with whispers

*There are no more customers*

Shadows flow over locked ornate wooden doors
creep up the delicate
filigrees of scalloped brickwork
discover the indolence of a leaning bicycle

The Lohar flexes his cramped hands
marvelling to himself
at the pulsating blood still
coursing webs
of ancient nicks and cuts

*These hands*
*These hands*
He says aloud to no one in particular

And is quiet

In time the hammer awl and anvil too
fall silent

*Exhale*

In neglect
in oxidation
mute unfinished metal shards
lavished with the attention of craft
smothered in burlap
are left buried and abandoned

In aging
beneath layers of molasses-stained dyes
they acquire exquisite
fragile patinas
the transformed primordial
waiting to inhale

When we move
we leave our hearths behind
and linger where we last breathed
our veins embedded in the clay
our sweat permeating obliquely into molten metal
where cautiously buried embers
are never fully slaked
beneath their blanket of fine ash

*Breathe deep*

I owe him this breath

# The Lives of Our Poets

## Waris Shah – *No Reprieve for Heer*

Midnight
and restless *Heer* awakens
    to familiar strains of fluted calls
        at her doorstep

Scanning the street
    she is confronted
        only with flickering oil lamps
        and the echoing of cobblestones
            the waves of the river Chenaab
            feverish in their homesickness for the sea
            heedlessly
        trace ever shorter downhill paths
    until spilling onto the forlorn pages
        of a poet's wet dream
            tumbling with each added accent
            towards the day's inevitability

Only, only, only… and only
    only the waves
        chanting the eventual dissolution into saline sea

My *Heer*
    it has ever been decreed thus
        no matter how skillfully nuanced your tale
        however tidy the sweeping arcs
            of water time fate
        each is doomed in its intertwined plotline
            to continuously tumble
                to pre-ordained conclusions
                downhill

It was ever such for *Heer* and her *Ranjha*
      no matter how you willed it otherwise
your fates sealed
      in the chainmail traversing his forehead
         the scribbles crisscrossing your palms
      in the sketching of your silhouettes
      and the echo of your profiles
         where each ordained sunny afternoon
         is limned with deep blue dusk
            and the scented promise of intimacy
Thus and thus and thus
      this day will ensnare
         the hapless *Ranjha*
            his willful *Heer*

*"The orchard songbird does not sing*
*Eternal*
*Nor is rapturous Spring*
*Infinite*
*Nor the blessings of*
*Parents*
*Beauty*
*Youth*
*Nor the company of friends"*

*The above quotation was extracted from Sayful Mulūk by the Punjabi poet Mian Muhammad Bakhsh (1830–1907)*

*Note: Penned by the Punjabi Sufi poet Waris Shah in 1766, the popular fable of doomed lovers Heer and Ranjha is the Punjabi equivalent of Shakespeare's Romeo and Juliet.*

## Mirza Ghalib – *Let There be Mangoes*

*In memoriam—Urdu poet Mirza Ghalib's 225th birthday (1797–1869)*

It is 1857
and the first Indian uprising against the Englishmen
        is in full swing

The Urdu poet Ghalib
        languishing in a pauper's cell
laments
        the loss of royal patronage
        the sorry state of fine verse
        the squandered opportunities for drink
        the loss of companions
                and more pertinently
        the lost seasons of mangoes
inscribing
        *Let there be mangoes    and lots of them*

Despite his state of insobriety
the lilt of his verse and wit come to us
        as if penned yesterday by a mischievous uncle
                who lives down the street
who notes that
        *The world before me is a children's playground*
and
        *A pageant plays before me day and night*

Ghalib will not physically survive his demons
        nor the literary and cultural decay of his hometown
and will remain mercifully ignorant
        that none of his seven children will outlive his century
or that following the uprising
        the Muslims banished from their Delhi
        will not be allowed back for another two years
and that the East India Company's *gora paltan*
        the first of the armed European merchant raiders
        will wreak such havoc in their vengeance
                that they will stain the countryside
                with the abandoned dead and dying
        while they continue to pillage
                whole continents of proffered goodies

Although the prowling goose-step march of history
      has not stilled just yet
the mango orchards thrive
and Ghalib's verse endures
      the ink on his parchment still wet

*Note: "Gora paltan" is the "white man's army."*

## Rabindranath Tagore – *Wilfred Owen Recites Gitanjali*

Even here
amidst rustling fields of parched poppies
and the receding of dews
the lotus blossoms
into monsoon clouds

We time the lilt of distant Howitzers firing
each salvo a physical blow
each barrel
owning its heartbeat
each fiery tongue
straining the stars with
familiar fables
of trench poets
who lace their bones
in the battlefields
of our assigned wars


*If the end comes here*
*Let it come*
*When I go from hence*
*Let this be my parting word*
*That what I have seen is unsurpassable*


*After his death at the Sambre–Oise Canal crossing at the war front in 1918, poet Wilfred*
*Owen's mother received back his personal possessions.*
*In the notebook that Owen carried in his pocket, he had copied Poem 96 from Gitanjali*
*with the author Rabindranath Tagore's name.*
*Owen had recited the lines from the poem quoted above when bidding*
*his final farewell to his mother.*
*He was only twenty-five.*

# Faiz Ahmed Faiz – *All Night Long I Watch Stars Drop*

*In memoriam—Urdu poet Faiz Ahmed Faiz (1911–1984)*

*On March 9, 1951, Faiz was sentenced to death and spent four years in prison before being released. A recipient of the Lenin Prize, he died in Lahore in 1984, shortly after receiving a nomination for the Nobel Prize.*

Once
a mere spoken word
        threatened to set us all free
so it was forbidden
and when that first word became a verse
        a sentence was imposed

Now there is only this cell
this cell by decree
has six impermeable walls
        one to stand on
        the other to cower under
        on another will hinge a one-way door
and the fourth
        this one opposite me
        will hold up
        a patch of black and blue sky
            torn from the fabric of my skin
            and hung out of reach
            this high to dry
Though out-of-sight solitary
        does not permit touch
through these bars
pours an afternoon sluice of sun
        that for eighteen minutes
        races across my upturned face
            *(A mere fourteen hundred heartbeats*
                *a condemned man will count anything)*

On the other side of the fifth wall
        is an open garden
I have not seen it yet
        it wafts to me on the evening breeze
and in this garden
        all are held in thrall
every blossom awaits your arrival
        leaves blooms morning-dews

I wait here all night long
        watching the stars drop
for me the beloved traces
        coded messages in the heavens
I imagine their caress on your face
        and follow dawn's pathway across your forehead
and thus I live and thus I die
with only wild imaginings to sustain me
where you and I
        bleed under the same sky

Across the sixth wall a madman
is tapping out urgent signals with his nails
        *we are all captives in a vast desert*
        *no leaves no blooms no morning-dews*
        *no scented evening breeze*
            *just buckets of sand*
            *littering every horizon with our delusions*
            *where even the mirages have long since evaporated*
        *learn to love the night*

But he mumbles a lot
        and all I may be hearing is the wind

And so my distant
        beloved and land
 I dwell a neglected night country
        where someone once buried my moon
        while another stole my constellations

I once slept in a snow well
I once slept in the arms of my mother
   and I have slept in the embrace of my beloved
I dig deep wells
   and crawl into their embrace
      searching for the sun
But wait now
   am I underwater
   or underground
am I grown taller by night
   or have these walls shrunk
is this the first year of my interment
   or the final fourth
am I still alive

Whatever it is
   listen to me for a while longer
   as I relearn to recite that first verse

   I know a word that will set us all free

## Sahir Ludhianvi – *This Man on Fire*

...is a whirling dervish
possessed by his jinns
he has forgotten his way home
and spews contagion along the way
stumbling across dimly lit stages
putting words in the mouths
of flawless silver gods
stretched taut
across the length and breadth of our walls

Until
there comes a day comes when his whispers
begin to percolate into our dreams

His mantra in this life
will be to connect with our deepest longings
even if it takes him a hundred deaths
and a hundred rebirths
and even when his process is controversial
the lilt and pace of his verse
is never uninformed
his tenderness never less eloquent
and his outrage at the human condition
never less infuriating
and soon enough this too becomes persuasively ours

His unfiltered poetry comes to us
his spell-bound-listeners
in all its purity
pungent astringent coy
always more potent
than mere literature
mixing the sacred with the irreverent
the prosaic with the divine
in the freshly perfected medium of playback

of such fluency
that it becomes the soundtrack to every season of our lives

Somehow he pierces
       the fourth wall
even as the trope-laden onscreen melodrama
       sinks under its own weight

**Defying Gravity**

Millions of listeners encounter him early
       not yet fully realizing who he is
       or what he is saying
imbibing from him their first inklings of humanism
       and recoiling from the sudden awareness
              how suffering is truly universal

Whether raga influenced
       or scripture sourced
these deceptively simple folk tunes
       with their soaring vocals
       and orchestral crescendos
              defy gravity
beguiling us into freefall

And so the listeners sit day and night in the dark
       spellbound and motionless
              sighing laughing weeping
              all at once
and occasionally clapping
       and tossing coins at the screen
When the lights are finally turned on
they do not wish to return to earth
       or for their euphoria to end just yet
and they set out to feed this newfound addiction to words
       wearing out scratchy needles
              on bakelite and vinyl grooves
       tangling magnetic tapes
       depleting radio batteries
and in the process stumbling upon the magic of *auto-repeat*
       long before there is such a thing
              as *auto-repeat*

**In the Spotlight**

When Filmfare fanfare accolades and awards smile upon him
empowered by this fanbase
is it any wonder that he contends
henceforth
      film scores will be composed for *his* lyrics
      rather than *his* lyrics composed to match the score
and he insists
      that he must be paid a *rupiah* more
      then the leading singer of the day
          a singer who has publicly proclaimed
          *film is just an excuse for music*

He declares that hereafter
      all radio stations broadcasting film songs
      must also credit the lyricists
thus revolutionizing our lyrical landscape
that must now acknowledge its creative sources
      and place the lyricist on the same footing
      as the playback singer and the composer

**Seeking Love…**

Given our cinema's twin fixations with Love and Death
and the long history of men sitting in the dark
      watching brightly lit women
there can be few real-life happy endings
      and his is to be no exception

When the beloved comes calling
      in the form of a fellow poet
the stuff of legends manifests itself
      as the eyes of a poet adoring from a distance
and we encounter him as tormented
      and at a loss for words as any one of us
      unable to directly resolve his affliction
      or express his inner turmoil

Jarringly
he becomes just another one of our silver screen's
      perpetually stricken
      morose lovers
      whiskey soaks
      serial tea-drinkers

and afflicted chain-smokers

When the two finally meet
they gaze into each other's eyes
          briefly exchange a few words
and unable to bridge the gap
          between two *mere* mortals
what follows can only be silence
The gulf in-between widens
until the absences and silences
          become insurmountable
so that after the final break
she will relive their brief shared history
by retrieving the smoked stubs left by him
          and pressing them against her lips

However
          alone once again
they do *not* drift apart
but begin addressing their life's work to each other
launching monologues on air and onscreen
          in the hope that the other is listening
thus reaffirming
that life is not merely an effervescent sum of
          a seven-year silence
          a pocketful of oblique glances
          a dozen exchanged love letters
          a cup of tea
                    from which the beloved last drank
          and the stubs of a lover's discarded cigarettes

After all had the man himself not reminded us
                    obliquely
                    *mein pal do pal ka shayar hoon*
                    *I am only a poet of these few moments*
          before adding barely an hour later
                    *mein har ek pal ka shayar hoon*
                    *har ek pal meri kahani hai*
                    *I am a poet of every moment*
                    *In every moment is my narrative*

## ...And Finding Death

In Love as in Death
a fortuitous mix-up takes place
       on the way to a writers' conference
the lovers' name tags are wrongly assigned
       and momentarily the poet becomes his beloved
         and she becomes him

It is not recorded whether the error was swiftly corrected
       However
when death does finally come seeking
       one born *Abdul Hayee*
         at his Punjabi birthplace
       a red sandstone haveli in Ludhiana's Karimpura
it does not find him remotely close to home
       and searches for the tormented youth in Lahore
       and then briefly for the restless poet in Delhi
         before claiming him
at his Bombay retreat of *Parchaiyaan*
       in a pall of smoke and alcohol fumes
       shattered and utterly spent
       once again totally at a loss for words
having already lived several lifetimes
       in a paltry fifty-nine years

Three decades later
       to make room for fresh interments
his tomb is unceremoniously demolished
and his mortal remains dissipate
       irretrievably
       yet somehow fittingly
by then
       *Sahir* the wizard
       *Sahir* the *banjara*
       *Sahir* the man on fire
has already escaped his mortality
       whether doomed or blessed
much like his inspirations
       Mir Ghalib Iqbal and Faiz

to become ours wholly in perpetuity
in the bonded embrace of our *dukkha*
> he tirelessly returns to us
> to relive past infatuations

**Today**

a century to a day since his birth
if death were to come looking for one named *Sahir Ludhianvi*
it will find a million-strong bearing his name tag
> stating
> *I am Sahir Ludhianvi*
>> *Come take me*

*Basti basti parbat parbat   gaatha jaye banjara   le kar dil ka iktara*

## Bashir Ali Lopoke – *While All of Punjab Sleeps*

This land of the *sufi sadhu sant faqir*
of generations of poets
of lovers and madmen         all asleep
and the five rivers leisurely chasing each other's tails
      from the Himalayas to the seas
      pausing only to sing the land to sleep

Yet where shall we lay our weary heads?

In fitful sleep I continue to dream of fires
fires that are still burning in the surrounding mountains and valleys
this rusting metal bucket is on fire
the fire consumes this pretend city of *One-couver*
and this pretentious dominion of *Kanada*
the fire also consumes the premature
      as well as the stillborn

While all of Punjab sleeps
a Raven picks my heart clean
      and spits out chewed bones

Icarus
the first of kleptomaniacs
      only craved the sun
falling in a tangle of furious wings
      his heart too full of thievery
          yet reluctant to settle
            for dirt
            for flights of imagination
the worm turning beneath his breastplate

Icarus sighs

My head is reeling from too much
      Tagore Whitman Rumi Ghalib
even the grass blades are beginning to stir beneath my feet
I hear the wind keening off the water
I watch ravens descend onto scraggly pines
and the familiar lines of ink in the handful of treasured books
      accompanying me on my voyage
      have suddenly become muddled strangers

I must now learn new skills
Rumi has whispered flight instructions
    *Learn to fall*
    *And in falling learn to soar*

# Midnight on Turtle Island

During the third quarter of the night
a Raven delivered us onto
the shores of Turtle Island

We arrived
inked in melanin
immersed in full body rash
our black and blue tattoos
chronicling our diurnal entanglements
and everywhere we looked
lifeblood was red
and everywhere we saw
there was light spilling
bending around edges
and everywhere we looked
*all living things were in a state of worship*

and *all living things were worthy of worship*

Exploring our bright shiny world
we squint like all new arrivals
unsure if the pith of our faith will still hold true
and sustain us here
we taste pine needles
stumble upon pungent intermediaries
of sawdust smoke ash sweetgrass
and everywhere we bump into the unfamiliar
hearing the wind sighing
as it practices new words
that litter the forest floor
or we decipher messages scribbled onto hillsides
that spill into rivers inlets seas below
and we comfort ourselves with the words

*we are stewards of this earth*
*for us all living things are in a state of worship*

and we seek comfort as *stewards of this land*
*for us every living thing is a companion*
Eventually
we learn how direction is paramount everywhere
we grew up praying to the west
and now cut loose from the lodestone

must recalibrate our compasses
to a *Makkah* that is now in a truer north
and as close as the heavens above

what I learned early from my grandparents still holds true
*there are seven directions*
*of the medicine wheel*

*north east west south*
*up down center*

*I can pray anywhere*
*the spirts of our ancestors are everywhere*
and in whatever we seek
direction is paramount
in the ritual of *Tawaf* we circumambulate seven times
counter clockwise
and across our seven skies
the number seven *expresses a multitude*

and like our Cherokee brothers
*seven is the actual number of the tribal clans*
*and seven is the number of upper worlds or heavens*

Observe how it is universally true
that no one who has ever been forced to go hungry
will fast willingly
yet during our month of *Ramadan*
from sunrise to sunset we embrace fasting

and as part of our long-standing spiritual practice
some in our communities also fast sunrise to sunset

on this first day of our arrival at school
we swallow our mounting panic
and focus on the single observation
that this door clanging shut behind us

is of yellow cedar
and no matter what happens to me from here on
i must remember this
while i can still taste the word on my tongue
before it is replaced by *wood*

and that this door clanging shut behind me
is of polished *himalya deodar*
and no matter what happens to me from here on
i must remember the taste of *himalya* and *deodar*
before these are replaced by wood

daily
new arrivals are led into this abyss
by those who call themselves
*fathers mothers brothers sisters*
and we wonder if they have children all their own
why *do* they never visit them
and would they treat their own this way

later
we stumble upon the lone figure
of a white bearded man
hung high in each of the 24 rooms of the building
whose outstretched arms
must be so very tired by now

at night i seek refuge in a cramped attic cubbyhole
that allows me to stand and pray
even if i can do nothing about the direction
for *we may stand and pray anywhere*
*for us the whole world is made a masjid*

and for us *all truth comes from our missing elders*
and *our misplaced land*
at dusk the downpour startles

hurling pebbles onto our slanted roof
and my head is crammed with words that dare not spill
for every whispered thought in mother tongue
will be promptly punished

*be calm* you remind yourself
*on other days dawn pours down this same roof in gentle rain*

i chant
*keep open your heart*
and let the spirits in
but never forget
never forget that when they stole our lands
they also stole our parents
our brothers our sisters
silencing us for good measure
by cutting out our mothers' tongues
they slashed our drums
dismantled our longhouses
forbade the potlatch
and sowed disease in our midst

one of our elders who saw this coming from far away
added particular poignancy to what we would endure
by whispering under his breath
these children
these children are not your children
they belong to the ages yet to be
these children
are arrows launched from your bows
*that land who knows where*
*these children*
*are life's longing for itself*

here we stand now
daily bearing witness
that all the 24 men hanging from these walls
have their eyes shut tight
they do not wish to bear witness
to what goes on here
while the shadows of our passing generations
maintain vigil on the other side of the wooden door
circling this e-shaped house of concrete

and daily we stand here and bear witness
pacing the 6059 steps from solitary
to one-way entry door
as hours turn days to nights
months to years

and daily we spend a lifetime here
yet we did not ask for this
our parents did not willingly send us here
they did not wish this for us
we were snatched from our mother's laps
and have been miserable ever since
our homesickness is a fever
that will not break

during mealtimes the fathers sit
on a raised dais
beneath an image of a mother sheltering her infant
and before each meal they call upon *their* father
who is art in heaven
to bless their food
and though we cannot see what they eat
it cannot be the same gruel served us
i whisper *bismillah* and dig into the turnips
i bless the spirit of the creatures who gave up their lives to be on this table

eventually
our neglect will teach us
that nothing we say or do
will amount to much
or change anything
and that all our beliefs are inferior
our souls in need of saving
our skins dirty

for now the walls of the boarding school
are as solid
as the walls of the residential school

*yet* we shall escape these walls
in wooden boxes
the length and breadth of our bodies
where the chinks between the planks
will be like the barred classroom windows

and everywhere we will seek it
light will bend towards us
already i dream of my brothers and sisters
gathering in clans beyond the trees
they sail giant canoes
fish hunt trap
tasting salmon in the running waters
and deer on open hillsides
they light giant fires to guide us home
and organize elaborate feasts
for our arrival

we shall escape
*we shall escape*
even if a century of night
must pass
before the digging begins
to set us all

*Free*

Today

We do not wish Our past on Anyone else
We shall undo this whitewash
*observation contemplation meditation instruction*
will set Us free from all Our locked exits
Our stories will once again be openly shared around Our fires

Now

In this open air gathering of all Our tribes
We have begun the process of healing
chanting *dhuas* making offerings
fully cognizant
that Our every act is significant
Our beliefs precious
Our skins beautiful

Come and see

How Our experiences have transformed Us
come and witness how We are now
*Bears Beavers Loons Muskrats Ravens Salmons Turtles Whales Wolves*
reclaiming reforming rebuilding
Turtle Island
in all its seven directions

# The Monopoly of Ink

*To those who stole my mother tongue*

*and to those who will not let me rage*

John Berger:

*"Never again will a single story be told as though it's the only one."*

A Punjabi expression:

*"Annah vanday shireeniyaN   te par par bukkaN khaye"*

*When the blind distribute sweets   they stuff themselves first*

# The New Nabob Only Drinks Yak Milk

... and only eats peacock meat
　　　　flavoured with crushed pearls
walks on rose petals
　　　　in the shade of silk parasols
where his every waking moment
　　　　every whim
　　　　is responded to instantly
　　　　*or else*
there is the choice of garrotte scaffold whip

In late afternoons
　　　　when the master rises from his siesta energized
he will clap and proclaim
　　　　*there was a cold day*
to mimic the local phonetics for *open the doors*
or he'll yell
　　　　*there was a banned car there*
and the doors will promptly be shut

He has been heard to mutter
　　　　*local vernacular is such a bitch to bother*

If the *pankhawallah* holding the silk parasol
　　　　looks a bit apprehensive
　　　　this early in the day

it is because his master awoke last night
        in beads of sweat
and found the one person
        whose sole job in this life is to tug on an overhead pulley
        of a fan arcing out of the master's bedroom
            blissfully snoring
and now the stench of delayed retribution
        stains the air of this stiff and barefoot triptych
        posed against a painted background

Rising swiftly from grocery shop attendant
        to overseas railway clerk within a decade
        so very distant from his puny local shire
a dozen right nods have landed him
as the new District Railway Inspector
        of an Indian neighbourhood
        the size of Wales
the new Nabob already owns a well-appointed bungalow
staffed by a retinue of fifteen servants
        including a buffalo attendant
        a keeper of the grounds
        even a pastry chef
        and a pair of feckless *punkhawallahs*

When he arrives in his personal railway carriage
        for a station inspection
the staff drape him in marigold garlands
        that stain his starched garments a merry crimson
and they pluck daisies
        to wilt in soilless flowerpots
and decorate his pathways
        red white and blue
        with crushed brick and limestone
        and sky pebbles

Rumour has it these days
        that the new Nabob is so very bored
and is seeking a mate
        to perfect his Nabobdom

# While the Fathers Feast on Mangoes with Knives and Forks

The seating dais raises their plates above our eye level

At the best of times
our boarding school kitchen strains
to serve 150 lunch and dinner plates
  of daily mutton served with potatoes or turnips
  lightly seasoned with salt pepper
  *(this week surreptitiously supplemented with wild mint*
  *someone must have stumbled upon the last wild patch)*
and for breakfast must rely on the economy of omelets
  where three eggs will feed five

Eleven years of patient coaching
  in etiquette
  the assigned lay of the table
  and the strategic positioning of each utensil
yet we need no formal instruction
on how precious are mangoes
  and how fleeting their season
and how there is only one way to enjoy a mango

  *use bare hands*

## English-ibajnuP

*Lord Thomas Babington Macaulay (1800–1859) famously proclaimed on February 2, 1835, "I have never found one amongst them who could deny that a single shelf of a good European library was worth the whole native literature of India and Arabia." To rectify this, he laid the material foundations of Western society in Asia, arguing that "We have to educate a people who cannot at present be educated by means of their mother-tongue. We must teach them some foreign language." His actions would lead to Macaulayism in India and the systematic elimination of traditional and ancient Indian vocational modes of education Punjabi would be its first victim.*

*However, ironically, today "Macaulay's Indian Children" celebrate his achievements on April 23 as the "English Day" for liberating them from the bondage of caste.*

### Borrowed Tongues

On this august day
How shall we celebrate the triumph of
Left margin-aligned English     over     *Right margin-aligned Punjabi*
You Germanic Latinized          *nayrA-odnI in detoor eM*
You gunmetal grey   &   *lios fo neerg eM*
Bastardized promiscuous porous  *devivrus evah htob ew woH*
You looted our word for *loot*
Then stole *chit dhobi chhota* from us
*ralloc zeemak noolatnap ruoy deworrob ew elihW*
*evig ot sruoy reven erew yeht hguohT*

Now

Where shall we finally meet?
If not in   *elddim ehT*
So that we can again to   *rehto hcae revo klaT*
Or be rude and familiar   *rehto chae tsap klat neve dnA*

Perhaps, one day  *ecarbme neve nac eW*

## Punjabi Offers Only One Word for *Shore* and *Thorn*

    …as if their lure and stab
could be contained in a single utterance
      *kunday*
yet redolent as mulch
the fecundity of this language of the soil
does not permit transmutations so readily
      into what is for me a third-hand tongue
      a Latinized mongrel
         all gunmetal grey
            too much crackle
            not enough whinge

On non-linear paths
Punjabi's temporal slopes become muddied
      into the strictly contextual
*kal* is both *yesterday* and *tomorrow*
*aajao*—a literal *come* and *go*
      means only *come*
and here the sound and fury
      of both a menacing snake
      or an approaching thunderstorm
strike us as a whistling *shookar*

When the Sufi male implores his creator
      it is always in a distinctly feminine voice

In school our transplanted
      English language teacher
      Scottish Fr. Johnson
         who after a lifetime in the province
         spoke better Punjabi than his class
once stumped us all with the scribbled term
      *sarfe-naal*      *with frugality*
and when an 'Oriental' language scholar
challenged our fricative consonant sounds

he left disappointed
expecting to trip us in our sibilant articulations
we were instructed to annunciate
      *a railway station  a bus stop  a steamship*
however by then we were too far removed from our roots
      to oblige him with
      *a rail-why a-station  a bus a-stop  a-steamship*

It is said that the Brits did what they did to us in punishment
      for mangling the name
      *and* occasionally winning
      at *their* favourite sport
            *cirkit*

## Two Poems Titled *Monopoly of Ink*

*01*

The kleptomaniacs had always coveted
    the lilt resonance pitch
    of my speech
and left me unable to speak
    of their denouement
they cut out my mother tongue
    and left me theirs
it does not fit my mouth
    it pours lead into every ear
    it robs my dreams of colour
        instead of green sap rising
        there is now this grey metallic tang
          and the resounding of steel

Here all my rainsongs shrivel

How do I now
    speak to my mother
    or sing homespun lullabies
      to my unborn

How will I daily shape these stones
    to earn my keep

*02*

And
    now that my tongue has regrown
I speak hybridity
    and am of numerous minds
Here
    *Here*
        &
          HERE
And must now learn to break through
    this chokehold
    over ink
    over eyes
    over ears
    over mouths
where my cry begins as a whimper
    and becomes a scream that no one wants to hear
where oceans of ink are spilled
    to tell *only* one story over and over
      everywhere
        forever

# ~~Entry~~ Exit Wounds

## *(Paar)*

*Paar: Punjabi for "across" or "on the other side."*

Artwork by Salman Malik

# ~~Entry~~Exit Wounds

*(In memoriam—Chin Banerjee 1940–2020)*

*Jis tara bund darvazoN pe gir-e baarish-e-sung*—Faiz


## *MOHAJIR*

## *PANAGHIR*

## *RAFIQ*

### *PAKI*

### *IMMIGRANT*

### *REFUGEE*

#### *WETBACK*

#### *FOTB*


It is midnight already

tell those

who hurl stones at my windowpanes

heed your words

**Go home**

## What's in a Name

*To an ex-colleague who suggested I change my name to one they could all pronounce.*


What's in a name anyway, Johnny B
      apparently a great deal

A sickly three-year-old
was the first child to be born in his extended family
      for nearly two decades
and following the grand tradition
the first name *Yahya*
was extracted from a randomly chosen page
      of the holy book
      *Yahya* is one of Allah's 101 names
      *Yahya* once meant "Yahweh is gracious"
      *Yahya* now means "it is also given by God"

When the child is still weak at four
the hakeem recommends
the child be bathed over a live snake
and the bath be followed by a name change
      *(the snake trapped under the wicker basket*
      *does not survive this telling)*
and when the finger falls this time
on the letter *T*
instead of the choices of *Tahir* or *Taufeeq* or *Taseer*
his parents choose the *aspirational Tāriq*
      *The one who awakens*
      *The one who knocks on doors*
and it was none other than that historical one
      who headed to Spain from North Africa
          and at the Gibraltar bawled
            *Burn all your boats*
            *there is no going back*
*The rock was not yet called the "Gibraltar," the name is an honorific "the Rock of Tāriq."*
*Look it up!*

Over the next fifty years of this child's life
various border guards and immigration officials
      to suit their formalities and vague inclinations
will mangle the order of the first middle and last names

until the boy now a man
        encounters a world
where they often ask him
        *What's in a name anyway*
        *if we can't pronounce it*
        *we can't know it*
        *Go change*


So *Tāriq* is now anglicized to *Derek*
it facilitates job applications
eases awkward introductions
        and more pertinently
John B and his colleagues can now pronounce it

(BTW, *John*, I have just learned that *Derek* is the English language short form of *Diederik,* the Low Franconian form of the name *Theodoric,* an old Germanic name meaning of "people-ruler")

So *that* is what's in *my* name

Let me tell you what else I have learned
        *Yahya*
            the name that made me so sick in early life
            when I didn't know any better
is also a variant on *John*

Now let me ask you this
        what is a *John* to you?

## Shadeism or Just Like Us but With Better Tans

How did this latent incident of melanin
this accident of birth
this fiction of my frictions
become my father's past
my present
my children's future

If I peel this subcutaneous layer
and cut to the bone
will I then see it layered
oozing spice and turmeric
if each cell recognizes a foreign body
is otherness cell deep
skin deep
bone deep

What is darker now
the contents of my full heart
the dilation of my dark pupils
coursing of this corpuscular blood
surging of these electrons
firing of these dendrites

Over shared drinks
my retired octogenarian neighbour
reveals with a disarming smile
the nuances of shadeism
*...do you see*
*do you see Derek*
*how we never trusted the darkies...*

Today
how do I dare now
to venture into the sun
if not to be made dirty
and
whole again

## On the Turning Away

September 11, 2001

On a perfect day like this
      I too
would choose to fall in grace
through the azure stretched tight
from our horizon to theirs
the world held in thrall
      time stalled
the universe lingering at the precipice
      of this one frozen moment
      before the turning away

As a young boy
I once reflected a sunbeam
into the murky depths
      of an unlit weed-choked garden well
         and discovered within it a cosmos

Since then I have gone through life
probing wide-eyed
      and in shock
akin to that of the sweet water salmon
first encountering the salinity
      of the open sea

And my universe has continued
      reluctantly
         to unravel

Forever impatient with shadows
traversing the sluice of my sunlit days
I have learned to tread cautiously
      on the crown of grass
      cresting my father's grave
having once seen a sparrow

fall from the sky
and stiffen at my feet
in a single wing beat

At other times I have woken from deep slumber
to the unbridled laughter
of my infant children
and have heard my beloved
hum to our unborn child

Between the shock of blue
and the blinding light
now the gurgle of that laughter
the lilt of that song
surfaces

Some of us have chosen to go headfirst
arms rolled backward
graceful as egrets plunging
I glimpse a figure flow past
clutching a purse
while a couple leaps in eternal embrace

High above the disbelieving crowds
how can I avert my gaze
there are a million Polaroids
witnessing
my sky torn asunder

How do scraps of flayed paper
pierce steel beams

Where and when and how
did we visit such fury
upon those who did this to us

# A Billion Ships of Theseus

What compels every seventh person you meet
to abandon their home
and join the jostling billion
to whom only denied shores beckon

Every refugee migrant asylum-seeker
is a veritable ship of Theseus
suspended between hearth
and a destination
that is not home quite yet

What do we know about this seventh person
thundering out to shore
mud-smeared hearth-less
ears ringing with the familiar and tired
generational arguments
pockets stuffed with ashes
of forgotten ancestors
the *Ghadari baba's* still sing
of breathing in the dust of my homeland
the dissolved bones of my elders

The ground shifts underfoot
and our armadas begin chanting
every delivering tide
and here
amongst abandoned harvest fields
freshly mined nocturnally
how quickly migratory herds have learned
to feed on hoof
while testing the integrity of barbed wires
with every savage tongue

Just last week
a stowaway casually tumbled
out of an astonished English sky
and landed on airport roofs
in snapshot rigor mortis
another spilled from an unclaimed suitcase
navigating an Arrivals baggage carousel

Perhaps
we are all such unclaimed baggage
endlessly circling
global carousels

## On Reading Renee Sarojini Saklikar's *children of air india*

I feel [redacted]
two prime ministers have offered condolences to each other
one from Canada the other from India
Your Excellency, I am sorry for your loss
I am also sorry for *your* loss
No, *I* am sorry for *your* loss
No, really, *I* am sorry for *your* loss

Far beyond this failure to communicate
stretches a magnitude of ~~im/~~personal tragedies
      and the weight of tears
      proliferating indolence impudent scrabbling
fungi obfuscations
      suffocate the air
~~these are cover-ups of cover-ups~~
~~where vital texts/evidence/recordings/testimonials~~
are made to ~~go missing~~
~~are withdrawn~~
until the well-oiled wheels of bureaucracy
      fall off

2:31 a.m.
In the victim/s mind/s
a tangle of details surfaces
      what was the source of
      cordite funds bribes
      strategic distractions
      ~~mis/~~directions

All the diced roti bits strewn in the thickets
      still remain
no ravenous feeders stumble upon them
      no sleuths pick up the trail

Cold case      Cold case
Move on      Move on

Each of the perpetrator/s
      move/s on

Only word/s linger/s
      and the victims
            how will they move on?

# Raising Nineveh

*Banished from our house in Kuwait during the first Gulf war, when we could carry our*
*belongings no further while crossing over into Turkey from Iraq,*
*we tore our family photos out of their picture frames.*
*A handful tossed currency into the waters below.*

So
here
we were
in the north
Iraqi border
town of Zakhu
a name and place
that we had not heard of
where our displaced refugee lines
begin snaking through ancient valleys

Around us whole towns have been razed
in acts of retribution
when a tyrant gases an irksome dwelling
and bulldozes all its inhabitants
only the mute tile work of the floors remains

Within our refugee tent walls
his ominous presence bled into our nightmares
his shadow looming
across the fractured landscapes

Urgent messages swirled
keening on the wind
for those who could read them
stretched taut across rusted barbed wires
echoing other histories

*Ancient armies have crept*
*through these fissures*

Twisted molten stones attested

*The wells are poisoned*
*the fields salted*

*You cannot stay here*

*You are not the first*
*to pass this way*

*Nor the last*

# X Marks the Spot

Cartographic dotted lines connect
Point A to B
Point A in Punjab
to Point B in *One-Couver Kanada*
15,000 miles apart
Now only 1,500 impossible feet away
the shore

And Point X
from midstream stranded ship
to beckoning shore
was that on any map
factored in some overlooked equation
marking the point
of isolation exhaustion
and midstream exclusion

'X' marks the spot
where a battle cry once echoed
where rust bled into water
and interlaced with salt
'X' marks the spot
where grown men wept
for the soil beneath their feet

Yearning
the deck heaves
against its anchor

I am that chosen raven
delivered
amongst this flock of your prized pigeons
I am the bunker coal
tossed at the shiny people
hurled at their threats

mine the salt sprinkled into your salinity
mine the blood spilled
clawing grasping
at land's edge
where saltwater encounters sweet water
and mingles with melting icebergs

Here freshwater
numbs the returning salmon
until they bump into objects
and offer up their bounty
gathering strength for the next assault

*(In celebration of poet Sadhu Binning's contributions to the teaching of Punjabi language in Canada)*

## The Sea Lion – Still Running on History

In marking the five-generation deep
        origins of our people
we repeat only two stories
        one of the loss of a paradise
        and the other of a vessel denied
                every beckoning shore

Landlocked Punjabis
        have always been bound
        by the sweet waters of snowmelts
and unable to swim across brines
        they must rely on singular leaps of faith
                to cross the widest of chasms

This one time
        unyoked from their oxen
they leaped across the darkest *Kaala Paani*
        wider than any river in flood
        even further than any living memory of waters

Until it came time for them to set foot on land again

Today
where minnows stipple the water's surface
an anchored rust bucket
was held captive for sixty days
        and nights
those chants have long since been silenced
their demands diminished
        and now this water holds no echo
                no memory
the waiting
the wringing of hands
the shouting
        has finally subsided

Yet
this *still* remains a crime scene
and the culprit is *still* at large

A century of lapping waves
and yet your veneered cladding of cedar

                is none the worse
your brass furnishings
        glint flawlessly in the sun
that signature steam whistle
        with which you menaced us for so long
                has long been muted
and the roving eye of the searchlight
        that kept us awake for sixty nights
                has gone missing
the shattered glass panes have been refitted
the decks scrubbed clean of spilled blood
the water cleared of bobbing police helmets
and the lobbed cabbage head
        once mistaken for an explosive
is nowhere in sight
and somewhere in the depths below
lie the hurled bunker-bricks
        and Japanese coal
        and hand-whittled missives
                hewn from Burrard flotsam

Moored so securely
        to this sheltered and peaceable shore
you float ethereally
        sparkling in this April sunlight
the gentle heaving and falling of your prow
attesting to your lone survival in our midst
        in awaiting indifferent paying customers
now for a few dollars anyone can hitch a ride

Like me
        you are still running on history

Yet your quaint presence in our midst
        rankles
        and I recoil inwardly
the hurt has not yet fully healed
yet only *you* can reconcile this century-old rift
        in our interrupted journey

I remain stranded in this host body of water
        suspended in Time and History
still pining for the denied shore

        *Come and fetch me*

# Wherever I Am

Today we stand on ancient burial grounds
like those distant and exquisite artifacts
buried and lost in the courtyard of my ancestral home

In this very building
several others are waiting to exhale
ancient timbers that should disintegrate to mark time
are here preserved for eternity
for us to gawk at

And now if you ask me
*… but, where are you really from*
my reply is
*I am from everywhere you are from*

*Like you I came here from Africa*

**40,000 years ago**
heading north by northeast
I thundered out of a continent
to discover another

**15,000 years ago**
in pursuing the woolly mammoth
and southwards receding warmth
I leaped across ice bridges and descended
into these raw and unformed mountain valleys
shields fjords and grasslands

**100 years ago**
my ship rounded Brockton Point
and came to an abrupt standstill
yet continued gathering steam for the final push
Now here we all are
sprawled across the rusting decks
our bloodlines stretching a century back
to this single day
anxiously peering over our shoulders
at what might have been

Mercifully
hidden behind the western horizon
is what awaits us at Buj Buj
the first deafening volley has already been fired
in the first imperial war

Our protests
have been silenced
and our silences can no longer echo here
Yet
twice daily the tides ebb and flow
cresting in exhalation
the crescent waxing
waning into the night

The fate of all tides is to turn
and return
will not this rising tide
lift my boat as well as yours

We were left tugging at this anchor for another **53 years**
before the floodgates to this Eden
finally opened

**5 days ago**
I crossed several imaginary dotted lines
descending into the Arrivals lounge at YVR

**5 hours ago**
my car rolled over the speed bump at the Blaine-Vancouver check post

**5 minutes ago**
I stepped off the ferry

I should be home by **now**

Yet
I am not fully there

Just a week from now
on 23 June I shall clear the final **1500 feet**
between creaking ship tugging at its anchor
and beckoning denied shore

I shall finally wet my feet again in the Pacific
and kiss this hallowed ground
and hug this shore

and then

only then

shall I belong

**wherever I am**

*Note: Extracted from the keynote address delivered on the occasion of Komagata Maru Centenary in 2014 at the Royal British Columbia Museum, Victoria, BC, Canada.*

# Why We Are (YVR)

*Vancouver International Airport (IATA: YVR, ICAO: CYVR)*

*For Robert Dziekański,*
*whose last desperate and fatal act of defiance was brandishing a stapler at the airport*
*security.*

### YVR here @ the Portal of Arrivals

At this first portal
we enter into
an imminent penumbral world
where our exhalations are held in check
the future will not be born
if the current world is not receptive
no heralds announce our arrivals
there are no more vacant concavities
into which we can be extruded
gasping clamoring
blue in the face
arriving only at this
our moment of birth
in panic mode

### YVR here @ the Portal of Departures

We may have arrived alone
but here we emerge at the other end
only to slip away
unnoticed
but escorted
handcuffed branded
invisible barriers ensuring
the two ends never meet
and whatever happens to us
in the interregnum
will always take place
behind tinted glass

# Who We Are

And now…

**Madja Rajic**
a young Croatian recent immigrant recalls
how after two whole homesick weeks
of Canadian winter
in a seedy Marpole and 71ˢᵗ
Vancouver Welcome House
wrote back home

*We have already seen Canada*
*Can we head back home now?*

And failing this plea
how she and her sister plotted
in the hope of arrest and deportation
to toss a brick
through a lit window display
and thus be repatriated
back home to their family

And now…

**Mikhail's mother**
visiting from Romania
having witnessed such bounty
displayed on the local supermarket aisles
pleads

*Let's return to the store*
*There is still good food left on the shelves*

And now…

**three-year-old Zain Zaffar**
snuggled next to his visiting father
on annual furlough from Kuwait
follows the overhead arc of a plane
and waving at the sky
whispers to himself

*Bye bye Papa*

# ~~In~~Visible Exit Wounds

…so now everyone knows…
*exactly* who I am
*this one-part human*
*three quarters a creature*

Always a *Mohajir* in India
a *Panaghir* in the Punjab
summoned by Kuwaitis
as their familiar *oye Rafiq*
the Brits beckon *oi Paki*
the overly polite Canadians
merely avert their eyes
from their *Immigrant/Refugee*
and cross over to
the safer side of the street
while the Americans gladly
underpay their *Wetbacks*
as long as everyone knows
who is *Fresh Off The Boat*

Is it just me or Everyone else
who knows exactly
where I belong in this
grand order of things

And why Everyone knows
the worth of my sweat
always precedes me
even when I am
~~In~~Visible
I

# Epilogue

## Fault Lines

*"Our sea has run out"* – nineteenth-century Indian scholar on the devastation and exploitation wreaked by their colonizers.

After ruling India for nearly two centuries, the hasty departure of the British from India on August 15, 1947, resulted in the division of British India into two independent dominion states, India and Pakistan. The Partition primarily involved the division of two provinces, Bengal and Punjab, based on district-wise non-Muslim or Muslim majorities.

The provinces of Bengal and Punjab had historically been foremost in their unceasing challenge to the British rulers, and these provinces also bore the brunt of the resulting hostilities.

The Partition displaced between 10–12 million people along religious lines, creating overwhelming refugee crises in the newly constituted dominions. There was large-scale violence, with estimates of the loss of life accompanying or preceding the Partition, disputed and varying between several hundred thousand and two million. The Partition's violent nature created an atmosphere of hostility and suspicion between India and Pakistan that plagues their relationship to the present.

(compiled with sources from Wikipedia)

2022 marks the 75th anniversary of the Indian Partition by the British.


"When kleptomaniacs decamp…
…you check your pockets for lint
you toe the coin in your shoe
you weigh the antimony in your beloved's eyes
her *bindi*
her silenced anklet bell"

# 1954

Over a series of summer afternoons,
a seven-year-old boy repeatedly bounces his taped tennis ball
against a stain on a smooth patch of a courtyard wall.

Eventually, the grimy whitewash begins to peel,
revealing a radiant mural bordered by an unfamiliar script.

When he confronts the adults on his find
he is met with a strange mix of mockery, denial, and even abuse.

By the following day, the mural has been freshly whitewashed.

## Encountering Terra Nullius

Embarking from one
      wet convulsive wind-swept
          and isolated isle
you came armed with the unshakeable faith
      in your musket sail book thought colour
and confident that all you traversed
      lands streams rivers seas oceans
were immediately stripped of their original
         peoples names ownerships histories
and rendered *terra nullius*
      no-man lands awaiting your christening
         in celebrating your various inbred monarchies

There was nothing left for you to learn
as you proceeded to encircle the globe
      calling it your personal granary
you planted nothing
      yet harvested endlessly
         and in every season
      with such ferocious greed
         that the scorched lands groaned
           *Our sea has run out!*

With your pantries overflowing
      and your armories bristling
the bully with the stick
now set out to civilize the world
the vagaries of winds
      and the fate of tides
would deliver you to my shores
      where we were too polite
      to reject your offer of cheap trinkets
         and welcomed you with open arms

Our ensuing home invasion
      would last a hundred thousand nights
until the day the bully would lose his stick
      and could no longer civilize us

We are still trying to awaken
      from your unleashed nightmare
and come to terms with this subcontinent-sized hole
      you left in our futures

## The Blind Cartographer

Did you know
that when kleptos decamp
they follow time-honed protocols
        for all such denouements
and that amidst the well-thumbed pages
        of the Colonizer's Playbook 101
        are detailed instructions
        on how to hastily grasp the elements
                gather up the skies
                divert waters
                dig deep the dirt
and then deposit these spoils
        into the well-manicured hands of
        their ever-attentive and on-the-trot
                the clueless blind cartographer


Who
        when tasked *to get on with it*
                hesitates


He is nudged gently
        *C'mon divvy up the spoils already*
        *The monsoon waits for no one*
        *You will personally never have to set foot into the fray*
        *We have even dotted the areas where the barriers are to go*
*and you will have nothing to*
        *conjure out of thin air*
*think proportion*
        *dissect bisect trisect*
*and remember it must all eventually fit into*
        *these three sturdy suitcases*
                *one very large*
                        *two much smaller ones*


And as instructed
        the cartographer begins his task
        by sharpening his pencils
        and testing the scalpel against his thumb
                until it draws blood
then arbitrarily hacking his way
        through thickets of intersecting tangles

he quantifies every unit
        qualifies each asset
wondering who has ever been tasked
        to apportion a sky
        or count souls
        where no one stands still

He toils nonstop for a day and a night
before deciding to
        bide his time till daybreak
when he will emerge triumphantly
        from his darkened room
        and pointing at his tangle of scribbles
announce to the world
        *This* is where *your* sky will end
        *This* is where *your* waters will break
and this
        *This* is where
        *Your* earth will be uprooted
           till the end of time

But wait
        there is to be an overnight change of plans

At dawn when it comes time
        to finally trace out the sheer elegance
           of porous dotted lines
        and drip his ink
           across our sky water earth
he is still stumped
        for no matter how he tries
        the elements do not hold
           the skies continue to leak
           the waters overflow
           the land bleeds soil
              onto the lavish carpet
Until
        he throws up his hands in disgust
           proclaiming

*This task I knew*
        *was never going to be easy*
        *the elements were constantly shifting*
           *troubled by shared histories*

*and intermingled bloodlines*
*communal ties*
*they coalesce interlace entwine*
*their roots run deeper than dreams*
*and no one does my bidding anymore*
*oh how these shoots are interleaved*
*the ash of these hearths*
*still too hot*
*to human touch*
*I cannot undo overnight*
*what millennia have interwoven*


And he stuffs his soiled gloves into his pocket
locks the door and walks away
remorseless
if he is ever troubled by his complicity
then only by the stained carpet
and the dirt and blood that have crept
beneath his fingernails


Ever since then
between our every hearth and outer door
there is a fresh splash of whitewash lime
where stray dogs guard the split
and the sky is stained
with a tumble of dots and dashes
beneath which no one dares to stand


Still

# When Kleptomaniacs Decamp

...you check your pockets for lint
you toe the coin in your shoe
you weigh the antimony in your beloved's eyes
       her *bindi*
       her silenced anklet bell

Here she is
flashing her creaseless palms
       *Look*
       they even stole our fortunes

When kleptos decamp
they take what they covet
       but do not really need
knowing that what they have not unmade
the survivors will undo
       with bare hands
       and unleashed tongues

Afterwards the village was full of gossip
from the rape of our land
       two stillborn
       sloughed off
someone screamed
       *Shame*
others tossed stones
someone tore the roof over our heads
while the perpetrator
salivating at other cataclysms to mete
       departed tactlessly
              100,000 nights too late

Come summer
       with rivers overflowing their banks
our washed blood
       enriched our harvests

Eventually
like every migratory flock
       we have learned
              to abandon our tampered nest

## Ammiji's Letter to Keshaliya

*Keshaliya was a childhood friend and next-door neighbour of my ammiji, who vanished with her family during the nights of the Partition. Ammiji spent the rest of her life regretting that the two had not said a proper farewell.*

I did not see or hear you leave
        my dearest Keshaliya
        that night of the troubles

How can I tell you
        *how can I tell you*
                *what has come to pass*
someone somewhere drew a line
and said everyone on that side
        is now your enemy
someone gave us flags to wave and said
        *You are free*
        *go and celebrate*

And *you, Keshaliya*
        were on the wrong side of this wall
*You*
who on the day of my wedding
        rode with me in the palanquin
        accompanying my collection of ragdolls
                on the way to my in-laws

*You*
who would always bring the ingredients for our *kujian*
        and then joke
        *I come from the house of merchants*
while I who brought the fire labour and breath
        would retort
        *I come from the house of Lohars*

On the eve of separations
        exhausted by too much memory
I too fell asleep
        and dreamt
a sequence of nightmares
        of blood staining our streets
        of violence behind the veil
        of screams within four walls

I dreamt our neighbours
      had invaded our home
      knocking down
      the slim shared walls
      that held up our common roofs
I dreamt
      and I dreamt
      and whimpered
      and cried
      until my screams awoke me

I found the streets stripped
      of the trilling of children
      of the footfall of grownups
      of the murmur of women at the doorstep
and I was greeted by echoing silences
      populating our uneven narrow streets
and no one dared fill
      or mention the void

Where are you now all my childhood friends
      *O Keshaliya*
      *O Surinder Kaur*
      *O Mala*
      *O Sarasvati*

Wanton and sated
      guilt-free
we slithered into your emptied courtyards
      to occupy
and further obliterate
      every sign of your presence

And Keshaliya
      you remember the precious mural
      in your courtyard
          of Krishna cavorting with the milkmaids
          and the flowering petals of Om
can you believe that the first act
      of the one who moved in there
          was to whitewash it

And how
to silence your continued echoes in our midst

we even melted your brass temple bells
into mute hammers and sickles

We silenced yesterday

And yet
somehow through this carnage
the *tulsi* has continued to blossom
      in our adopted courtyards
and rains have pelted the fresh whitewash into submission
      revealing the cowherd's flute again
      and the Guru's hand raised in blessing


Your laughter had died on
      these streets
yet our walls still echo
      to the trilling gurgling
      of your hide and seek
and the lingering strains of *mahiya* and *Heer*
      still move us to tears

You left behind such renewable bounties
your rooftop Aloe vera
      mends our children's paper kites
      as well as our casual wounds
in the season of wind-tossed mangoes
      there remain unplucked silent orchards
      that no one now has the heart to harvest

And now
as the stained Chenaab in flood
      dissipates into our fields
the *koel*
      still heralds the rains

We were pagans then
      and we are pagans still
floating earthen lamps
      into floodwaters
lighting *diyas* on mausoleum walls
marking our harvests with carnivals
lining our eyes
      with antimony

staining our foreheads
      with lamp ash

My friend
some days
      when I put my ear against your wall
      I can hear you
            playing hopscotch

Old habits die hard

## *Batwara Batwara* – The Partition Story

**A Play in 75 Years (August 14, 1947 to 2022)**
     … three generations late

I watch a dozen children play out the Partition story
as six boys gather around their stick game
     of *gulli dhandha*
the girls at their clay pots
     of *kuji*

When a tall boy traces a line in the mud with his thumb
     the others reinforce it with their fists
they build a rudimentary wall along the line
they divert a river
     reminding each other
     *slap anyone who crosses over*
they raise huts on either side
     attaching to each roof a thatch
they split their animals roughly
     someone gets the left hind leg of goat
     another a chicken's stringy innards
a sewer is let loose to flood enemy lines
when a fly buzzes across the tear
     it is promptly pounced upon
and when a crow dares to wing it out of sight
     it is brought down with slingshot
     the mummified remains strung up in warning
the boys anoint their foreheads with blood
pat each other's shoulders
and upon inspecting the sharpness of their barbed wire
     call themselves men

The two groups of girls exchange recipes
     split the *daal* evenly
and set up fires on opposite sides
     bringing their pots to boil
when one notices they have forgotten to salt the rice
     and seeing the boys preoccupied
she steps over the line
     and borrows some from her neighbours

I continue to watch as the women first feed the boys
       until they are quiet and calm
so that when one notices the wall he had built
       he hastily demolishes it
while another rakes his fingers blurring the lines further

Only then do the women sit down to eat
and over food they exchange gossip
       staring into the flames of their hearths
       and smiling at their children playing at
              *Batwara Batwara*
       the boys at their *gulli dhandhay*
       the girls at their cooking pots of *kujian*

All these boys were angry men once
       when nothing made sense
so that if one called out to the other
       the only response was a hurled insult or missive
       even when an inner voice whispered
               *Stop*

Then one day we learned that out of nothing
       something emerges
       even when we cannot comprehend it

We who were all such boys and such girls once
       once

We for whom
       *kal*
       means both *yesterday*
       and
       *tomorrow*

We who can barely survive our *todays*

## Reading "Midnight on Turtle Island" on Page 53

This poem was written for presentation at the Islamic History Month Canada's Theme 2021: *Anti-Indigenous Racism and Islamophobia: coming together for a month of healing.*

*Turtle Island* is a name for Earth or North America, used by some Indigenous peoples in Canada and the United States, as well as by some Indigenous rights activists. The name is based on a common North American Indigenous creation story.

My work attempts to trace very broad and subjective parallels between two belief systems, at least in their similarity of ritual and spirituality, while avoiding all performative aspects of this exercise.

*Midnight on Turtle Island* is a shaped, concrete poem, where the visual aspects of the work are as important as its contents, and my challenge was to present three different narratives in a single flowing piece.

To do this, I have relied on the left-aligned musings from a boarding school attic; while the right-aligned monologue offers a view from a residential school dorm floor. Both the experiences eventually merge in the middle.

Since part of the narrative takes place during the dark century of the night, I have chosen to present that section as white text on a dark background, where even the pronouns remain uncapitalized.

# Parting Thoughts

If I write with agency and confidence, it is because I stand on the shoulders of giants, our Canadian poets of South Asian origin: Kuldip Gill, Sadhu Binning, and Ajmer Rodhe.

I humbly acknowledge that this work was written by an immigrant settler on the traditional, ancestral, and unceded lands of the following nations that have welcomed us here:

Musqueam, Squamish, Tsleil-Waututh, Kwikwetlem, Katzie, Kwantlen, Matsqui, and Sumas of the Stó:lō nations.

My immense gratitude to the care and attention to detail that this book received from the team at Caitlin Press; I wish my earlier work had also been handled by their very capable hands.

A specially warm thanks to our local poet Christopher Levenson for his many inspirations and generous guidance, and for graciously penning the Foreword; to the many early readers of this poetry trilogy who participated in its final shaping and offered valuable guidance: Tohmm Cobban, Ted Slater, Sultan Somjee, Surrey Muse's Fauzia Rafique, and SFU's Betsy Warland. I also owe a deep debt to the late Punjabi poet Laeeq Babri for his spare blank verse and early redirection towards poetry. And, finally a nod to the prolific online elegance of Andrea Cohen's lean work—each has shown the way.

A very warm thanks also to Dr. Prabhjot Parmar (UFV) for early encouragement and guidance throughout in compiling these poems.

I have also credited our inspirational South Asian historical poets by assigning to them a section all their own: *The Lives of Our Poets*. For anyone left wondering who the poet Bashir Ali Lopoke is, he is the fictitious protagonist travelling to Vancouver on the doomed Komagata Maru voyage, as chronicled in my novel *Chanting Denied Shores*.

The use of non-English words throughout my work comes naturally to me as they are gleaned from the various cultures I have physically inhabited, namely Punjabi, Urdu, Hindi, and Arabic. Even when the intrinsic "other" resists all our attempts at absorption, it nevertheless insists on being woven into our narratives' larger canvas; I have retained some without recourse to translation/transliteration where I felt the contextual essence had been sufficiently conveyed.

This book initially began under the working title of *Nights of Kleptomania* before switching to its current title that serves it better.

Different versions of a few of these poems have been published in my earlier works, namely *Rainsongs of Kotli* (TSAR Publications) 2004, *Chanting Denied Shores* (Bayeux Arts) 2010, and in the anthology *Unmooring the Komagata Maru* (UBC Press) 2019 as *Still Chanting Denied Shores*. A version of *A Billion Ships of Theseus* appeared under Verbal Art (GJPP) 2019.

August 14, 2022, Vancouver, BC, Canada
All comments are welcomed at *derektmalik@gmail.com* and Twitter @TariqMalik0_0

## About the Author

PHOTO SALMAN (SAL) MALIK

For the past four decades, Vancouver-based author Tāriq Malik has worked across poetry, fiction, and visual arts to distill immersive and compelling narratives that are always original and intriguing. He writes intensely in response to the world in flux around him and of his place in its shadows.

Born in Pakistani Punjab, he came reluctantly late to these shores. To get here, he first had to survive three wars, two migrations, and two decades of slaving in the Kuwaiti desert. He firmly believes his passion for distilling the alchemy of light/chroma/pixel, and his bouts of furious thinking about life and words in general, can all be happily and gainfully combined. He loves landscapes, bodies of living water large and small, and readers and listeners, and claims he writes so that he has something to read to his tribe on Open Mic Night at the local Poet's Corner or on the hallowed grounds of local public libraries.